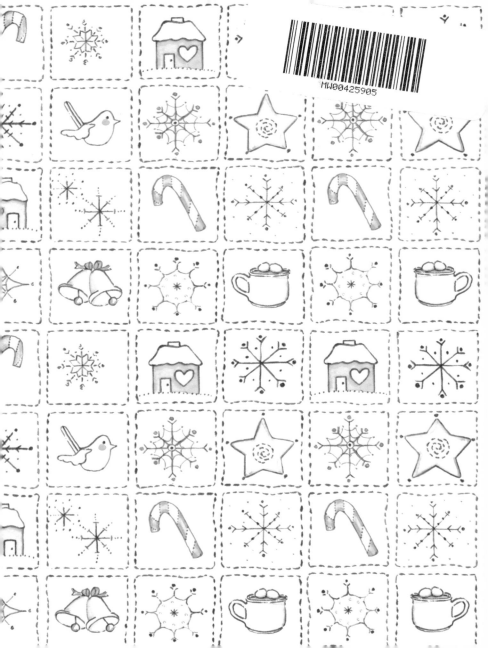

MW00425905

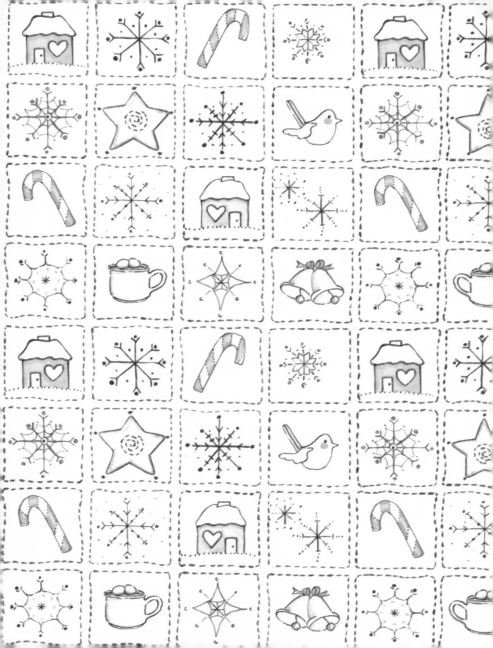

Home for Christmas

When I grow up, I'm going to write for children, and grownups that haven't grown up too much, all the earth songs I now do hear. ♥ Opal Whiteley

MyBook

SPRING STREET Publishing

MARTHA'S VINEYARD·MASSACHUSETTS

Copyright 2020 by  Susan Stewart Branch
ALL RIGHTS RESERVED

In accordance with the U.S. Copyright Act of 1976, no part of this book may be reproduced in any form or by any electronic or mechanical means, including scanning, information storage & retrieval systems, & uploading without permission in writing from the publisher, except by a reviewer who may quote brief passages in a review. For permission, contact:

Spring Street Publishing
PO BOX 2463
VINEYARD HAVEN, MA
02568
sales@springstreetpublishing.com

FIRST EDITION
ISBN 978-0-9960440-5-9
Library of Congress Control Number
2020941251

10 9 8 7 6 5 4 3 2 1

LSC-IN
PRINTED IN THE
UNITED STATES OF AMERICA

To my
Mom & Dad
& my brothers
& sisters
with all my
dearest love. ♥
And to good
moms & dads

everywhere.
You are the
heartbeat &
backbone of
the world. ♥
We'd be nothing
without you (in
more ways than one.)

And to everyone committed to
keeping the magic alive. ♥

Love is Forever

For we need a little music,
Need a little laughter,
Need a little singing, ♪
ringing through the rafters~
And we need a little snappy
Happy ever after,
♫ Need a little
Christmas
Now~

♥ Jerry Herman

Forward

How am I to sing your praise,
Happy chimney-corner days,
Sitting safe in nursery nooks,
Reading picture story-books.
♡ Robert Louis Stevenson

Books meant the world to me when I was a little girl. As the oldest of eight children, "alone time" in our house was hard to come by. But it didn't matter, because I had books and the real world disappeared when I was reading. My four brothers could be practicing their wolf-howls in concert with our dog and the baby could be hungry and letting the whole world know about it, but I'd never hear a sound, I was so engrossed in the adventures of the March family, or learning how to play the "Glad Game" with Pollyanna. Reading was like my secret power.

LITTLE WOMEN

So you can imagine how thrilled I was last Christmas when my seven and five-year-old nieces asked me to read them a story. I chose a small illustrated children's book, published in 1938, I'd found in a used bookstore. The girls nestled in beside me on the sofa next to the lighted Christmas tree in our old house in New England, built in 1849 by a whaling captain ～

a house forever smelling of pine and ginger and woodsmoke from all the Christmases over the years.

The little book I chose for the girls told the tale of a grandmother describing to her grandchildren what Christmas was like when she was young, a passing of memories that took us back in time. I've aways loved stories of life in the "olden days," hearing the jingling livery of a horse-drawn carriage, the sound of long skirts sweeping the floor, a teacup settling into a saucer in Emma's garden . . . it's the closest thing to time travel I know.

So there we were, the three of us together, enjoying a Christmas of long ago.

Wide eyes watched and little ears listened as I read and turned the pages, showing them the pictures. My eyes filled with tears while reading the author's memories of her father's candlelit church on Christmas Eve, her brothers and sisters popping corn on the "jolly stove" with the isin-glass eyes, and especially the way the story ended, when she opened the cover of the book she'd gotten for Christmas and read a familiar passage:

6

"The rooms were very still while the pages were softly turned and the winter sunshine crept in to touch the bright heads and serious faces with a Christmas greeting." ♥ Louisa May Alcott

Ahhh, the nostalgia. The sparkles in my niece's eyes told me they felt the magic too even if they didn't understand some of the old-fashioned words. The Christmas we were reading about had taken place over a hundred years ago, and yet we were right there, stringing popcorn in front of their fire, helping to blow out the candles on their Christmas cake.

This got me thinking about our Christmases in the small house in California where I grew up. I was surprised to realize I could tell what Christmas was like over 65 years ago (yikes!) ~ when we were still feeling the effects of World War II. Things were very different then; Winston Churchill and Eleanor Roosevelt were alive and well, General Eisenhower was President, and everything we had was made in America. Milkmen left glass bottles of milk on our porch, gas cost 30¢ a gallon and was pumped by a uniformed atendant. There were individual jukeboxes on lunch counters ~ for a nickel Elvis, Doris Day, Little Richard, or Buddy Holly would serenade you over your

7

banana split. At school we practiced cursive on huge blackboards that covered the walls, and lined up to get our polio vaccines. Girls wore dresses for everything, to school, for roller skating, hopscotch, and cartwheels, too ~ and every boy on our street had a six-shooter and a coonskin cap. Drive-in movies were wonderful, under the stars, the whole family went to see *Lady and the Tramp*, us in our jammies. We had rotary telephones and a party line, and this new thing in the living room called television.

I could be the grandma now and write a book to tell the story of my childhood Christmas, a fireside book that would turn the clock to yesteryear, a book that would ride the wings of time so my girls could tell their children.

And so I am.

Now I light a candle to write my Christmas story with paper, pen, and paintbrush and pretend I am Mr. Dickens and it is snowing and the childhood muses I remember so well dance around my drawing table like sugar-plum fairies. I'll light the fire, you bring your tea ~ sit close and let me tell you a story...The world was a blur to me then, but now, even the tiniest memories appear in intricate detail. I still hear my mother singing.

Back on its golden hinges the gate of memory swings ~ My heart goes to the garden and walks with olden things.
>~~> Ella Wheeler Wilcox

Once upon a time

Everything should begin
with a love story . . .

My mom and dad met at a
dance in the ballroom of
the Villa Riviera Hotel in Long Beach,
California in 1945. My mother was a
dark-haired, brown-eyed 15-year-old
named Patty Smith ~ her mom did not
know she was out. She went to the
dance with her classmate, who was
meeting her boy-friend, who brought
his friend, Jack Stewart, who was 22.
Both guys were just home from the war
and dressed in their Navy uniforms
which was thrilling for the two young
girls. A mirrored ball was spinning
from the high ceiling sending specks of
light twinkling across the room onto
uniforms and flowered dresses . . . my
mom and dad danced and the orchestra
played *I'll find that Dream*:

*Imagine me with my head on your shoulder,
and you with your lips growing bolder...*

It was meant to be. A year later, with blessings from their parents (and lucky for me), they were married. 🤍

My dad got a job with General Telephone, so they moved from Long Beach to the wide open spaces of the San Fernando Valley. That's where I grew up, along with my seven brothers and sisters ～ in a pink-stucco four-bedroom house my parents bought for $16,000 with help from the GI Bill.

Making Ends Meet

Our neighborhood was brand new ～ the streets were lined with young trees and look-alike ranch houses built for the growing population that came after the war. We didn't have a lot of money but just enough, apparently, because we had the basics, warm beds, clean jammies, friends, shoes, grilled cheese sandwiches, and parents who loved us. I always thought we were rich because I felt so happy.

What one loves in childhood stays in the heart forever. ♥

MARY JO PUTNEY

"Are we rich?" I asked my mom. "Not rich in money," she said, "but rich in love. We have each other. That's what counts." It was a highly satisfactory answer. It sounded exactly like "Yes."

Contentment is natural wealth.
♥ Socrates

11

My parents were children during the Great Depression. They knew hard times and saw waste as a sin. They were taught, and told us often, that "money doesn't grow on trees." My dad brought his paycheck home and gave it to my Mom. She looked for sales, collected coupons, made weekly deposits to the Christmas Club, sewed curtains for our house, and made clothes for us. She saved Blue Chip Stamps and cut recipes from her Ladies Home Journal that "served a crowd," but cost three cents per serving. When necessary, my dad took extra jobs, and my mom, too, would sometimes work evenings at a coffee shop to help pay for "extras" such as Christmas.

Try hard & never give up.
♥ John Stewart

12

What gave my parents confidence was their belief in the American dream. Their generation had pulled together with the rest of the world, fought a long war against a nightmarish threat, and won. After years of Depression and war, they yearned for security and a sense of normalness. They moved to the suburbs and had lots of kids, found a lightening of the heart, and happy satisfaction in simple pleasures.

Over and over we heard our parents say how lucky we were. "We're Stewarts!" my hard-working dad would tell his little homemade team from his seat-of-the-pants, take-charge, do-it-yourself point of view. His words made us a team, proud to be so many and to take up a whole pew at church. As children we had no concept of the wider world, we thought everyone lived just like we did at 6847 Claire Avenue, Reseda, California, USA, Western Hemisphere, World, Universe. As we know now, that wasn't quite true. Life wasn't always as simple for others in the 1950s. We really were lucky.

The secret of having it all is believing that you do. ♥

There were 53 children living in the twelve houses on our dead-end street, and more coming all the time. Our front yards, back yards, sidewalks, and streets for three blocks on every side were our playground for ball games, picnics, camp-outs, yo-yo competitions, roller-skating, hopscotch, variety-show performances, circuses, and lemonade stands. Our mom

helped us do any creative thing we wanted as long as it didn't kill us. Bikes made us totally mobile from about six-years-old. Parents didn't worry as long as we told them where we were going and were home in time for dinner. 💙

Each weekday morning our Greatest-Generation war-hero fathers walked out their front doors, tossed their sack lunches into Hudsons, Studebakers, Nashes, and Fords, and went off to work ~ while young mothers waved goodbye from front porches, holding coffee cups, wearing homemade rick-rack-edged aprons, surrounded by their fresh-scrubbed, milk-fed, baby-boomer children.

He's making a list, checking it twice...

I was nine in 1956. My mother was 26, and my dad was 32. I had four younger brothers, and the baby at the time was my first sister, Paula. Two more sisters, Mary and Shelly, were coming, but we hadn't met them because they weren't born yet.

Christmas was our favorite holiday, but it took forever to arrive. A snail was faster; a turtle was a racehorse compared to the hands of the clock in the weeks leading up to Christmas.

Things finally got going after Thanksgiving. The sun set earlier; the spicy smell of cinnamon and nutmeg wafted from kitchen windows; we made gifts in Brownies; and the commercials on T.V. told us Santa Claus was on his way. I thought about Christmas constantly, to the point of becoming unhinged (You have NO idea. I was a nightmare; I would burst into tears without notice).

The kids in our family were young and completely bewitched by the story of Santa and Mrs. Claus, the elves, the reindeer, and the brownies. It was almost too exciting, too much magic, too many secrets. My parents tortured us with their furtive glances at the dinner table, rustling paper, a door hurriedly opened and closed. What? Tell me WHAT? It was agonizing. Discussions with my dad at the dinner table as he innocently wondered out loud where Santa might be at the moment, or what we might do if he got stuck in our chimney did not lessen the delirium for his children.

I wasn't sure how direct my mom and dad's connection to Santa actually was, but I knew they had a lot of influence with him. Good little girls and boys would get a visit from Santa, but if you were bad? You'd get a burnt cookie (and a heart full of shame). There was a lot to worry about. The limp Christmas stockings hanging over the fireplace were both a promise and a threat.

Hurry Christmas, don't be late.
We've been good, but we can't wait.

I made my bed every day, rode my bike to the Piggly Wiggly ("the Pig") to shop for my mom, and came when I was called, good as gold.

I'd be sitting in the big green armchair watching *The Million Dollar Movie*. My mom would put the baby in my arms, wrapped tightly in a receiving blanket, ready to be fed. I tested the temperature of the bottle by putting a few drops of warm formula on my wrist.

I loved feeding her, burping her to sleep, pulling her blanket aside, seeing her tiny fingers curled around mine. My mom called me the "little mother."

Like mother like daughter ♥

Because I was the first child and the only girl for a very long time, my mother and I formed a homemaking partnership that we both loved. We were in it together. She was only 17 when she had me. We had everything in common — we both loved dolls, we both adored Shirley Temple and knew all her songs, we both liked to play Jacks on the kitchen floor. A glance from my mom was all I needed to know what I could do to help. I made her happy, and she made me feel important to her, which made me want to make her happy, which made her happy, and it went round and round like that for our whole lives. I was sure I would NEVER get a burnt cookie for Christmas, and I planned to keep it that way.

Oh noooo!

 THE TREE

My dad took the bigger boys to the mountains to cut down our Christmas tree while my mom and I waited at home with the little ones, watching and listening for their return. We sang ♫ *Kiss me once, and kiss me twice, and kiss me once again, it's been a long, long time* ♫ along with the radio . . . while we gave Paula a bath, put her, Chuckie, and Brad down for naps, hung diapers on the line, creamed sugar and butter, added egg, flour, baking powder, and milk to make Snippy Doodle, sprinkling it with lots of sugar and cinnamon so it it would be nice and crusty when it came out of the oven. We cleared and vacuumed the corner of the living room to make space for the tree.

Dad and the boys drove into the driveway like conquering heroes followed by the clamor of my brothers' friends who were playing dodge-ball in the street. The kids clustered around the station wagon chattering and trying to "help" while my dad untied the ropes and wrestled the tree off the roof, through the front door, and into the living room, radiating pine forest through the cloud of chill mountain air that came in with it.

18

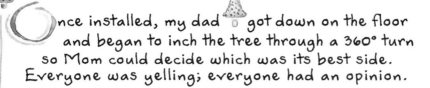

nce installed, my dad got down on the floor and began to inch the tree through a 360° turn so Mom could decide which was its best side. Everyone was yelling; everyone had an opinion.

"Quiet!" Dad ordered. He was almost completely hidden under the tree. "Let your mother speak! No one else! Are you ready, Pat?" My father ran a tight ship.

"I'm ready, Jack. Go ahead. Turn, turn, keep going, more . . . Stop! Let me look. Better go back a little. Back a little more . . . There!"

"Are you sure?"

"I'm sure! It's perfect."

We ate warm Snippy Doodle, crunching the sugar between our teeth, and watched while Dad looped colored lights round and round the tree, tossing crinkly-foil garlands over the top, down to the bottom, and back up. Then it was our turn. We children (and some of our friends) hung the striped and flocked Shiny Brite glass balls.

Mom put up the most precious decoration of all: great-grandma Orr's mercury glass, beaded-wire bird-house, a little bent, but still revered because it had come from my mother's childhood. My mom brought out the tinsel she saved from last year, tied neatly into bundles with torn up rags. We hung it carefully, one strand at a time (clumps of tangled tinsel were frowned upon in our family— by age four you knew you didn't want to be the one to do it). When my dad finally put the star on the top and turned off the lamps and plugged in the tree lights for the first time, it was almost unbearable-- it was so beautiful. My mom put her arm around my shoulders, pulled me close, and said softly with eyes bright and shining, the thing she always said, "Aren't we the luckiest?" We all agreed, THIS was our best tree EVER.

CHRISTMAS SHOPPING

Mom pushed the buggy with Paula and Brad inside. The rest of us followed along like ducklings into J.J. Newberry's Five and Dime. We trailed past the soda fountain, between the bolts of fabric, through the sewing notions and skeins of yarn; we bought Christmas cards in the stationery aisle, continued on to kitchenware, and stopped in the pet supplies to look at the goldfish.

The store was decorated in tinsel and ribbon and smelled like popcorn. The clerks were dressed like elves, and Joy to the World played on the PA system.

*O*n the toy department Mom and I admired the dolls while my brothers enjoyed touching and playing with almost everything else. The dolls were way up on a high shelf, where we couldn't reach. If we wanted to see one up close, we had to find a clerk with a ladder to bring it down. There were dolls with coiffed hair and thick eyelashes, baby dolls wearing sunsuits and bonnets that cried real tears, bride dolls all in white net, and ballerina dolls wearing pink tu-tus and satin toe shoes. And highly-coveted dolls with names like Betsy Wetsy and Ginny Doll, each with a wardrobe of clothes and accessories ∽ small refrigerators and electric stoves, doll beds, high chairs, and ironing

Stove is called "Little Lady".

boards were up there, too ∽ miniature champions of domestic bliss. Perfect for pretending.

"*O*oohh, Sue, aren't they beautiful?" said my mom, pointing to the dolls. "Which one do you like best?"

21

Clutching my hands together under my chin, I scanned the array. "Oh Mom, I hope Santa brings me a Terri Lee Doll." Every girl in my neighborhood wanted a Terri Lee, but only Janie Neilson across the street had one. I didn't really expect to actually get one. It was too big of a dream, too dear. I only wanted one.

"Oh, yeah," she said, nodding and looking up. "Look at that dress! Isn't it dreamy? How could anyone not want one! Her hair is the same color as yours! But wouldn't you rather have Tiny Tears? You could feed her like a real baby, with a real bottle! You could change her diaper!"

Slowly I dragged my eyes from Terri Lee over to Tiny Tears, because she was right; there was something quite alluring about giving a toy doll a bottle. "But Mom, I already do that with Paula, I want a grown up doll!"

"That's right!" she said with a laugh. "We already have a baby doll right here, don't we?" She was looking down at Paula asleep in the buggy. "The very best kind! Well, we'll just have to write Santa when we get home!"

Dear Santa,
We've been soooo good 💚.

Bobby wants a pair of skates,
Suzy wants a sled.
Nellie wants a picture book,
yellow, blue, and red.

CHRISTMAS IS FOR CHILDREN

In front, from left, Bradley, Mary, Paula, Chuckie ~
back: Stephen, Me, and Jim. One more, still to
come, our last baby (Baby Forever), Shelly.

23

Backward, turn backward, O Time in your flight; Make me a child again Just for tonight. ♥ Elizabeth Akers Allen

Santa Claus Lane

In mid-December we went on our yearly Christmas adventure that started with breakfast-for-supper ~ pancakes, crisp-edged and buttery, cooked in the big iron frying pan and swimming in maple syrup, with baked bananas, orange juice, hot chocolate and marshmallows, which we ate in our pajamas at the kitchen table.

After supper we bundled up ("Everyone go to the bathroom; put your slippers on. Jack, grab Chuckie's sweater. Stephen, where are your socks?"), and piled into the station wagon for a rare night-time drive across town to a famous neighborhood (a perfectly normal neighborhood at other times of year) where every house was decorated and brightly lit in a carnival of electric noise and color.

A bumper-to-bumper stream of cars, each filled with chattering, wide-eyed children glued to the windows, inched down Candy Cane Lane, over to Carolers' Way, up Frosty the Snowman Avenue, shouting in amazement at the make-believe winter-wonderland of sparkling lights dripping from houses with Rudolph-the-Red-Nosed-Reindeer mail boxes. Santa waved from his sleigh as reindeer paused on rooftops, elves danced on porches, bells rang, and carols played from loudspeakers. There were life-sized nativity scenes, including mangers with Mary and Joseph watching over the baby Jesus asleep in the hay, surrounded with wisemen, shepherds, camels, and sheep, with a lighted star over all.

The excitement of the spectacle wore us out. We fell asleep on the way home, and the little ones were carried blissfully from the car to their beds in the strong, cozy arms of our mom and dad.

Bells are ringin', children singin', all is merry & bright . . .

The bell rang at 3:10 pm on the last day of school before Christmas vacation, and we went tearing out the chain-link school gate, down the alley, across Tampa, past the Pig, three blocks more (careful not to step on any cracks), and into the arms of our mom, showing her the cards, construction-paper chains, bells, snowflakes, and handprints in clay we made in school. Freedom! For two whole weeks!

Our grandma was the main event of every holiday; nothing could happen without her, especially at Christmas. Mom and I started getting ready for her

arrival by cleaning the house. Secrets and sneaky gift-wrapping reached a peak. In the meantime, Mickey Mouse Club, Jack Benny, I Love Lucy, Bob Hope, Ed Sullivan, and Ozzie and Harriet had Christmas specials on television.

26

Home-Born Happiness...

There were rewards for being the oldest: one was that I got to stay up a little later than the other kids. After they'd gone to bed, the house was quiet enough to hear the clock ticking on the mantle. My mom was sitting at the kitchen table writing Christmas cards; my dad was asleep on the carpet in front of the T.V.; our dog Nipper was tucked up next to him, belly up, snoring softly. I turned off the T.V. and the lamp and curled onto the sofa under one of my grandma's knitted nap-blankets, listening to Bing Crosby singing *White Christmas* on the record player, with the lights from the tree blurring everything like a dream, until my mom came in and kissed my forehead, her soft brown hair brushing my face, and sent me to bed.

There's a dream that I dreamed of once in a lullaby...

It's Christmas in the heart that puts Christmas in the air. W.T. Ellis

ANTICIPATION

Whispering to my baby brother to find out if he remembered heaven. He was so fresh, his wide, blue eyes so clear, I was sure he could if he tried.

"Remember before you were born?"

"All gone," he said.

"No, not gone. Remember a long time ago?"

"No." His finger is pressing in his eye.

"Bradley." I pulled his hand down. "Stop, you'll put your eye out. Now think. Remember before you came here, you lived somewhere else, called heaven, remember? Remember angels?"

Looking up sideways, a bubble of drool on his lips, "Ain-juls?"

"Yes, remember? What was it like?"

"Cookie?"

Changing the subject again. He would not tell me.

Bring Out the Presents!

y mother was great at building suspense. Almost too good. Just as we older ones were beginning to jump out of our skins because Christmas was almost here and there were no presents under the tree, she quietly brought out a few carefully wrapped gifts, one for each of us.

"You can touch the one with your name on it," she said, "shake it if you want, but don't open it! We have to wait for Christmas morning."

NO PEEKING

hen she walked away and left us to our insanity. My package was about seven inches long, thin as a stick, weighing almost nothing. I examined it thoroughly, squeezed it, heard it clunk when I shook it. I laid my eye along the seam where the paper was taped together to try and get a look at the contents. I couldn't see a thing. She probably wrapped it in tissue paper first; she was evil that way. The only thing I could imagine it might be, I couldn't make myself believe, it was too awful.

Sue

TIED UP LIKE FORT KNOX

29

I handed it to my brother, Jim, who was eight and had an inner sense of such things.

"Here, what do you think it is?" I watched his face.

He squeezed it, rattled it hard, smelled it, handed it back, and said, "It's a toothbrush."

Me, my brother Jim, and our Mom's Circus Cake.

My heart dropped into my shoes. Oh, nooooo. Noooooo. Why? I was crushed. This was so close to a burnt cookie it wasn't even funny. Maybe worse. It was almost embarrassing.

*B*ut he was right. I felt it again, felt the oval toothbrush case and the edge on the cap right through the paper. When I squeezed it, the thin plastic case crinkled. The longer I fooled with it, the more I was sure it was a toothbrush. Nothing else it could be. It wasn't even like a Christmas present. It was like bathroom supplies. Who would do that? Tears rolled down my face.

*M*y mother smoothed my hair and said, "What's wrong, honey? You don't want a toothbrush?"

"NOooo," I wailed, inconsolable.

"You know, some poor little girl would LOVE to have a toothbrush."

30

Causing fresh tears that ungrateful me was stealing a toothbrush from someone who really wanted one, maybe even needed one.

"Don't worry," she continued, "I'm sure Santa will leave you something else. Maybe something nice. Wait and see!"

Sure-sure-sure, I thought.

"I know," I said, downcast and forlorn, searching my brain for the Pollyanna way of looking at this (there always was one but this was more of a challenge than usual).

The secrets did me in. The whole thing made me a 9-year-old nervous wreck. My dream of a Terri Lee Doll went into the "probably-not" column. That awful stick-package sat there, poking me, whispering "toothbrush" every time I walked by. Jim's knowing eyes taunted me. I ignored him and it and worried straight through to Christmas morning.

TOOTHBRUSH drummed in my head.

All the world is made of faith and pixie dust.
♥ J.M. Barrie

Tick-Tock...

The day before the night before Christmas . . .

By December 23, everything had to be perfect because my grandma and my uncles were coming! My mom and I (mostly my mom), dusted and vacuumed, shook out rugs, swept floors, washed countertops and cupboard doors, wiped down the stove and the fridge inside and out, cleaned the bathrooms, and folded fresh towels ready to hang at the last minute. There were clean sheets on the beds, our jammies were laundered and tucked into drawers, the tablecloth was starched and ironed, windows were washed, porches were swept, and there were ten new rolls of film on the kitchen counter.

We didn't have a guest room in our house. My bedroom had a double bed for me and a crib for Paula. Jim and Stephen were in one room; Chuckie and Brad were in another; my parents had the fourth. (By the time my next two sisters arrived, we would have to move to a bigger house. But that's another story.) When my grandma came to visit, she always slept with me.

"When is Grandma getting here?"
I asked for at least the tenth time.

32

DOMESTIC BLISS ♥

Mom was in the kitchen sterilizing baby bottles and filling them with formula. Peanut-butter cookies were cooling on waxed paper. A Tuna-Noodle casserole covered in crushed potato chips was just out of the oven and cooling on top of the stove. Paula was asleep on the bassinet in the corner of the kitchen. Bradley was in his highchair, kicking his feet and sucking on graham crackers and my dad was out back mowing the lawn. I had just finished turning the slices of bread drying on the ironing board for the turkey stuffing. The boys were on their tummies on the floor in front of the T.V. watching Crusader Rabbit. We were all waiting. Our grandma was the highlight of Christmas.

"**S**he'll be here in a little while. Why don't you take Nipper and the boys and go outside and wait for her."

She turned her head toward the living room and called, "Jim? Steve? Chuckie? Come get a cookie and go outside and wait for Grandma with Sue."

We sat on the curb in the California sunshine, eating our cookies, and waiting ~ chattering to our friends who lined up on the curb to help us wait ~ they were almost as excited as we were; they remembered her from last year. All eyes were on the corner of Claire Avenue and Hartland Street, hoping to be the first to see her car. My grandma was a legend.

And then...

Shouts from the kids could be heard for blocks when our grandma's Buick slowly turned the corner and lumbered into our driveway. HERE SHE COMES! MOM! MOM! GRANDMA'S HERE! Thrilled to bursting, we jumped up and shouted in the general direction of the kitchen window since we weren't about to go in-himself side now. Santa Claus could not have asked for a more enthusiastic welcoming party.

34

Everyone gathered at her car door as Grandma carefully pushed it open and stepped out. My brothers and I bunched around her, burying ourselves in her green-knitted dress, arms around her and faces turned up as she leaned down for kisses. My mom came out to greet her, "Mums!" ～ I was happily trapped between them as they hugged. My mom turned to us and sweetly suggested we calm down and give Grandma room to breathe. Dad came from the backyard. Nipper wound between his legs, his shaggy tail slapping back and forth.

The inside of my grandma's car smelled like her perfume, a mysterious, grown-up fragrance that was instantly recognizable because her house smelled the same way. The wide front seat was stacked with Tupperware filled with homemade treats layered on waxed paper: my dad's favorite peanut brittle, the frosted molasses cookies she made every year, and great-grandma Orr's powdered-sugar pfeffernusse. In the back seat there was a bag of apples, another of whole walnuts, a jar of bread-and-butter pickles, cans of black olives, a wooden crate filled with oranges, a box of ribbon candy, and a giant 18-pound turkey. My dad took charge of all of it, starting with the peanut brittle. But it was what was in the trunk of Grandma's car that we kids were waiting for.

By the time Grandma got around to the back of the car, we were giddy with anticipation. She put the key in the lock and turned to look at us with twinkling eyes. We held our breath as the heavy wide bonnet swung upward in a whoosh. The whole neighborhood stood on their toes and leaned in to look at the magnificence. A collective "ahhhh" floated like a cloud around the car. Her trunk was like Santa's bag, overflowing with colorful gifts, big ones, little ones, enough for the whole family, wrapped in Christmas paper, with dancing snowmen and silver stars, golden angels, flying reindeer, and candy canes tied with curled ribbons ⁓ so many presents, all of us had to help bring them in.

We skipped up the front steps of our house, carrying gifts, reading tags, giving each box a shake and a feel before placing it under the tree, then running back out for more. I was happy to see that not one of them looked like a toothbrush.

Toyland, toyland, sweet little girl & boy land...

That was a very difficult night for sleep.

See all the presents by the Christmas tree?
Some for you & some for me
Long ones, tall ones,
Short ones, too
Some for me & some for you. ♥

Christmas Eve Day

Mom and Grandma spent all day in the kitchen measuring, mixing, sifting, and stirring, getting as much of the cooking done for Christmas dinner as they could. I peeled potatoes and apples and rolled out pie dough. They made creamed onions, candied sweet potatoes, and Jell-O salad. By the time my two uncles arrived, the house smelled like cinnamon and apples and baking pies. My mom's younger brother, Dick, was 25, her older brother, Bob, was 27 and in the Navy ~ they came carrying gifts and bags and a box of our favorite See's candy.

The house was filled with Christmas joy and intoxicating expectation ~ pies cooling on the window sill, mistletoe hugs and kisses, tree lights sparkling, music playing, screen door slamming with the coming and going of starry-eyed kids. Grandma had her boys, Mom had her brothers. And we had our two uncles to tease and play with. Everyone was happy.

Faithful friends who are dear to us,
gather near to us, once more.

Dad hefted the turkey into the sink, rinsed it inside and out, dried it with a towel, and put it in a roasting pan. The men went to the garage to get the dining chairs down from the rafters, then out to the street to play catch with the boys.

We girls made my grandma's famous turkey dressing (the one she learned to make from her own grandma when growing up in Iowa) while singing along to the radio with Rosemary Clooney, Gene Autry, and Frank Sinatra ~ Christmas carols floated from our kitchen windows.

♫ Fa-la-la ♪
Frosted window panes, candles gleaming inside painted candy canes on the tree . . .

"Jack," my mom called outside, "Can you please come in? We need you to taste the dressing!" He was our official taste-tester.

Grandma put a forkful of dressing in his mouth, "What do you think?" she asked while he chewed, "More salt?"

"Yeah," he said, "a little more ~ you know turkeys steal salt from the dressing. You should always put in a little bit extra." He said that every year. My dad had turkey knowledge from way back.

Grandma winked at my mom and nodded, "Okay. How about more butter?"

Another bite. "Nooo, it's okay," he assured her, "it's good, it won't dry out." He waited a moment and said, "Can I go now?"

We asked the same holiday-cooking questions every year ~ as much a part of the sound of Christmas as Jingle Bells.

'Twas The Night Before Christmas...

Bedtime for the kids was early on Christmas Eve. It was the one night of the year we didn't have to be urged to bed. We knew Santa wouldn't come while we were awake.

I squeezed my eyelids tightly closed, willing myself to sleep, but my mind jumped all over the place: our house, my family, our Christmas tree, the stockings, the chimney which seemed so small, the surprises under the tree, will everyone like the presents I made for them ~ and of course I worried about Santa, how in the world did he ever get down that chimney? Thinking I might try to peek into the living room, deciding better not, there was something very burnt cookie about that idea.

My brain finally ran down, and I dropped off to sleep ~ muted voices, bumps and clunks crept into my dreams from the grownups, who stayed up late arranging things under the tree, snacking on Chex Party Mix, drinking egg nog, and watching Bing Crosby's Christmas special.

Above thy deep & dreamless sleep
the silent stars go by...

39

Christmas Morning

I didn't hear my grandma come to bed, but she was there when I woke up. She was a light sleeper, which was a problem for me on Christmas morning when all I could think of was getting out of bed and into the living room to see the magic that Santa brought (even though it was 4:30 am and still totally dark).

When I was little, she always caught me trying to escape ~ I would try to go slow, but at the last possible moment, quick as a jack-in-the-box lightning-bolt (with a hand on the end of it), she would reach out and grab my arm, her low, sleepy voice coming out of nowhere saying, "Where do you think you're going?" Yeeeiiiikkkkss! She'd pull me back to bed where I had to lay, wide-awake, obsessed, waiting for the sky to brighten, or for my brothers to come sneaking down the hall, whichever came first.

But this time I was older, trickier, and crazier than ever, and I had a plan. So carefully, there are no words for it, I began inching toward the edge of the bed as stealthy as a jungle cat, barely breathing, with uncharacteristic patience no one would believe.

I stopped after each tiny movement, waited a moment, listened for my grandma's breathing, then started again. I finally got a leg out, then an arm. My heart was thumping. This was the hardest part, it's where she always caught me. I could almost feel her hand closing around my wrist. If she spoke I knew my heart would leave my body. Every fiber of my being was on alert. I turned over incrementally in what I hoped might read as a "common sleep pattern of activity," until I was on my belly. I waited, then slid, soft as a rag doll, to the floor. And listened. I was on my hands and knees next to the bed — and my grandma was still asleep! Slowly, like you've never seen slowly before, I crawled across the floor, out the bedroom door, around the corner and into the hall. I paused, listening to the house. Nothing. Just my heart. I rose carefully, running my hand along the wall for guidance, and down the hall I went, on tiptoes, trembling with excitement.

Did he come? Did he? Did he?

I stood there peering into the dark living room, trying to get my bearings. The tree was a black mound in the corner, but the stove light from the kitchen sparkled the tinsel just enough to give me a directional hint. I tiptoed a wide berth around my uncles asleep on the sofas — if I wasn't careful, they would grab me and slow me down. And now Jim and Steve were in the room with me. Back-up. Strength in numbers. Nothing could stop us now.

We stumbled over our filled stockings, large lumps that Santa had arranged by our ages on the floor in front of the fireplace. There were shadowy shapes, maybe a rocking horse, something tall against the wall, something else like a chalk board, ∿ lots of unwrapped gifts from Santa Claus! I began touching things, trying not to disturb them, as I felt my way through the jumble of wrapped gifts around the tree. I found a face, a doll's face ∿ eyes, and a nose. I leaned in further to try and pick it up. I wrapped my hand over the top of the head and lifted straight up. I had it!

Suddenly, before I could bring it to me, the doll fell back to the floor, hitting the other Christmas presents with a crunch ∿ but the HEAD was still in my hand! I almost screamed. Had I broken it? It was too dark to see. I stood there, frozen, holding the head, on the verge of tears, thinking what my mom would say. A moment later my sadness turned to confusion that turned to slowly-dawning understanding . . . the thing in my hand couldn't be a head, it wasn't heavy enough . . . it was round like a head, but . . . my breath caught . . . it was a hat! An empty hat! Like going from zero to 60 in two seconds. If I wasn't 9 and resilient I would probably have had to go back to bed.

I breathed dizzily and reached back in to get the rest of the doll which was still in a sitting position, legs splayed out in front of her.

lifted her out, wrapped my arm around her middle as any practiced doll-mommy would do, stepped over everything, and took her to the window where the tiniest thread of pink light was beginning to edge the sky around my dad's plum tree. I sat down on the floor to look closely at the doll. My dream had come true. It was a Terri Lee, dressed in a Brownie uniform, just like mine. The hat? That I thought was the head? It was the brown felt beanie with a dancing brownie-elf on it, a miniature hat just like my own. She was perfect. I didn't break her. My cup runneth over.

Christmas Day

Dad came into the living room, already dressed, carrying Brad in his footie pajamas, Chuckie following behind. "Merrrry Christmas," whispered my dad.

"Dad! Dad!" Jim was beside himself, jumping on my dad, shrieking, "Look! Santa left me a two-wheeler!" Dad hugged Jim, laughing, saying, "Shhhhh."

"Me too, Dad!" Stephen hollered.

"NO WAY!" Dad said, realizing the time for quiet was over.

Dad plugged in the tree lights which set the room aglow. He lit a fire while his wild-eyed kids ravaged the area around the tree. The uncles began rubbing their faces and moaning, pulling their blankets over their heads.

Family Love

Mom came in carrying Paula. Brad wrapped himself around her leg and held on~ she laughed as she hobbled over to kiss my dad saying, "Merry Christmas everyone!"

Grandma, still in her robe, called out, "Good morning, Happy Christmas!" She patted the top of my head and asked, "You got away from me this morning! Did Santa bring you surprises?"

"Oh, yes," I cried, "My dream came true! Look!"

"What is it, honey?" said my mom. (She liked to hear us tell her.)

"It's Terri Lee! Look at her! She's a Brownie, just like me! She even has shoes like mine!" I was so happy, I didn't need anything else.

Mom fed the baby, Dad made coffee ~ everyone watched while we emptied our stockings onto the floor. "You guys must have been really good!" Mom laughed at her tousel-haired boys tumbling about in their Hopalong Cassidy pajamas, picking up yo-yos and paddle balls, bringing favorite things to her lap.

HO HO HO
MERRY CHRISTMAS

There were boxes of chalk and crayons, coloring books, paper dolls, and jars of bubbles ~ it was, "Look, Mom! Silly Putty!" "Look! A magnifying glass!" And me, with Terri Lee in my lap, "Oh boy! New barrettes!" Pick-up-Sticks, army men, Pez, socks, jacks, a penny for the gumball machine, and (always) an orange in the toe of each stocking.

While we played with the toys in our stockings, Mom and Grandma got dressed in their Christmas best and went to the kitchen, soon to be followed by my dad and, finally, my uncles.

It was barely 7am, but there was a LOT to do before we could open our presents. We had to get the turkey into the oven, have breakfast, get dressed, and go to church. "Quick as a bunny," my mom said. I don't know how my parents did it with so many of us, but they always told us, "Organization is the key to success."

While we put our stockings away, Mom and Grandma stuffed, trussed, and basted the turkey and put it into the oven. Dad made more coffee, poured orange juice, and opened a giant pink-cardboard bakery box filled with doughnuts from the Piggly Wiggly.

Christmas morning was the ONLY day of the year we were EVER allowed anything as extravagant as doughnuts (despite the fact that they were only six cents each). We all gathered around the box, trying to decide between glazed, crumb, or chocolate. Everyone in the warm little kitchen, drinking coffee and orange juice, uncles leaning against counters, Dad frying eggs and bacon, Mom and Grandma wiping sticky hands and faces, helping the little ones get dressed, everyone so excited, everyone so happy!

And He took the children in His arms, placed His hands on them and blessed them. ♥ Mark 10:16

Off to St. Joseph the Worker to hear Father Greene tell us the Christmas story. ♥

For to us a child is born...

46

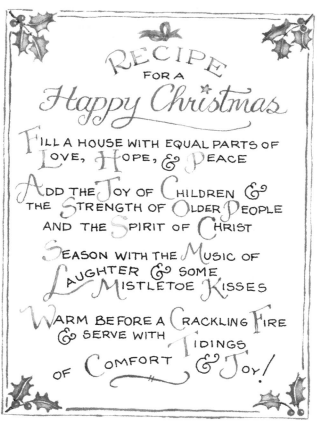

RECIPE
FOR A
Happy Christmas

FILL A HOUSE WITH EQUAL PARTS OF
LOVE, HOPE, & PEACE

ADD THE JOY OF CHILDREN &
THE STRENGTH OF OLDER PEOPLE
AND THE SPIRIT OF CHRIST

SEASON WITH THE MUSIC OF
LAUGHTER & SOME
MISTLETOE KISSES

WARM BEFORE A CRACKLING FIRE
& SERVE WITH TIDINGS
OF COMFORT & JOY!

We hear the Christmas angels
the great glad. tidings tell...

Gifts!

Finally, the moment we'd been waiting for. It was time to open our presents. We were all in our places, adults on the sofas and chairs, kids and Dad on the floor in front of the tree. Mom wanted to

You give me a book, I give you a tie, Aunt Martha always wanted an orange squeezer...
The Bishop's Wife

see everything anyone got ~ she wrote it all down, keeping track for the thank-you notes we'd write later.

My dad slowly handed out gifts, only two or three at a time. We had to be patient until our name was called. Squeals of joy, shouts of surprise, louder every year...

"**J**im and Steve, these are for you!" My dad handed Jim and Steve matching gift boxes.

"Wild Bill Hickok cap guns! Thank yooooou!" They screamed in unison, digging into the boxes.

Chuckie bounced up and down saying, "Ya ya ya ya ya ya ya ya"... so happy with his toy guitar.

"**W**ow," yelled Steve, "YES! Mom! A Pogo Stick! Who's it for?"

"It's for everyone, Santa brought it!" she said, "For you kids to share."

Look Mom! Look Dad! We vied for attention at the top of our voices.

48

"Look Mom! Mr. Potato Head!" Jim hollered.

"Cookies!" screeched Bradley, waving a cookie in the air. He loved what I gave him!

"A jump-rope!" I screamed, "Thank you, Uncle Dick!"

"Neato!" cried Jim pulling something out of a small box. "Thank you, Uncle Bob!"

"What'd you get?" He prompted.

"A horn! For my new bike!!!" He started honking it. Perfect, because what everyone needed was a little more noise in the room.

"A Girl Scout Handbook!" Inside I read, "To my darling granddaughter Sue, with all my love, Grandma." I jumped up to hug her. "Thank you, Grandma!" Surely dislodging the ear drum closest to my kiss.

It was all too much: everyone was whooping and hollering with joy. Paper and ribbons flew across the room to the trash box. Mom was folding all the good stuff to save for next year.

y dad got a box of Peanut Brittle all for himself. Mom got Tupperware popsicle-makers ~ she loved the hankie I embroidered with her name. Grandma thanked her for the Reader's Digests and the apron. The uncles whooped when they opened new pen knives and "rock and roll" 45's. Grandma gave us a Coleman lantern for our camping trips ~ and all the kids got new jammies.

Joy to the WORLD

ut it was the box of Terri Lee doll clothes my mom made on the Singer sewing machine in our kitchen that I loved best. My heart leapt when I saw the pink, dotted-swiss party dress with the teeny lace-edge at the neck and sleeves, and a full crinoline to go under it ~ and so much more:

a pink coat with lace to match the dress, a seersucker playsuit, a green corduroy shirt with red buttons and a pair of overalls, and yellow flannel jammies with bunnies on them. My mom. She made them at night after I went to bed. I jumped up and threw my arms around her. She just laughed. I couldn't stop smiling. It was just the best thing ever. (It still makes me cry to think about her doing that.)

And then, when it looked like we were done, when everyone was almost worn out from the jumping and screaming, kissing and hugging, my dad reached deep under the tree and pulled out one last present. He handed me a stick-shaped package that weighed almost nothing and was a little worse for wear.

The dreaded toothbrush had surfaced. I'd forgotten all about it. I glanced at my brother Jim who was watching me. I already knew what it was and felt no need to look inside. I hunched over, more or less to hide it, and tore off the wrapping paper . . .

Sue

WE DO NOT REMEMBER DAYS, WE REMEMBER MOMENTS.
♥ CESARE PAVESE

Christmas Blessings

I had actually come to accept it. A toothbrush wasn't the worse thing in the world. Who doesn't need a toothbrush? But I still didn't particularly want anyone to see me getting bathroom supplies for Christmas, especially not my brother. I already had the perfect Christmas. I pulled Terri Lee closer for strength.

"What is it, honey? Show everybody!" My mother.

I pulled the cap from the crackly plastic container and dumped it into my hand . . . and to my complete and utter astonishment ~ it wasn't a toothbrush! It was a PEN! I sat there for a moment in shock. Up-down, up-down, up! This Christmas might do me in!

Looked like magic to me.

"Oh My Gosh! MO-OM. . . ." It was a fancy, re-fillable, ballpoint pen, the top half had rhinestones (like diamonds) set in white enamel. The bottom was brushed gold, and it had perfumed blue ink that smelled like roses. A pen to go with the new box of stationery my grandma gave me. It was the frosting on the Christmas cake. I burst into tears, feeling a little sheepish. I held it up proudly, my cheeks pink with surprise and gratitude, thinking it was like art. "I love it soooo much, thank you Mom and Dad!"

Teary-eyed, I looked at my brother, triumphantly holding the pen up to make sure he saw it, but he just shrugged. Either way, toothbrush or pen, it was all the same to him, which is to say, not a B-B gun, not a slingshot, not electric football.

My characters shall have, after a little trouble, all that they desire. ♥ Jane Austen

Gift-opening was over, but not Christmas! There was so much more. Mom and Grandma went back to the kitchen to baste the turkey again, both wearing the new pearl sweater guards my dad gave them. The rest of us went outside to see our friends who'd been knocking at the door since 10 am trying to get us to come out.

The neighborhood was swarming with shouting kids in coonskin hats and sheriff badges having cap-gun shootouts between the houses, testing out new roller skates, doing Slinky experiments on porch steps, puffing on candy cigarettes, flying balsa-wood airplanes, and hula-hooping. Dad and Uncle Bob helped Jim and Steve learn how to ride their new bikes, running alongside them, keeping them upright, hollering, "Pedal!" Uncle Dick pogo-sticked down the sidewalk wearing Mickey Mouse ears, followed by laughing children.

By the way, while we are in this lovely place that no longer exists, as a voice from the future let me say, if there is a more satisfying sound than roller skates hitting the cracks in the sidewalk, I don't know what it is. Right up there with the screen door slamming on a beautiful day. And the mouth-watering smell of Christmas dinner wafting from your own front door. ♥

The glad and golden hours...

Gather to the Feast

Christmas dinner started at 4 pm at our house. We ate in the dining room which was a rare thing ~ that space was normally reserved for the playpen. But Christmas was special and the playpen was folded up on the porch. The two uncles opened the leaves of our very old dining table. Grandma and I spread it with the white damask tablecloth my mother had ironed. The centerpiece was a glass bowl filled with shiny red apples. I helped set the table with Tupperware, plastic, Melmac, or flowered china for each setting, depending on your age and station in life.

Dad came in from taking out the trash, "Mmmmmm, smells good in here! When do we eat?"

"It's almost ready, call the kids, honey . . . then come back ~ it's time to carve the turkey!"

"Sue, will you feed Paula? Maybe we can get her to sleep through dinner. Jim and Steve, go wash your hands. And please, somebody take that kazoo from Chuckie. Who gave that to him?"

Bob turned to her with twinkling eyes, took off his wax lips, and raised his hand.

Rolling her eyes, she said, "You nut. I won't forget this when you have kids."

"Here, Jack," Mom said, holding a spoonful of gravy to my dad's lips. He stopped carving and opened his mouth.

"Yum, that's delicious. More." He pointed to his mouth, open like a baby bird.

From my grandma to my mom and always in our kitchen, and now, in mine.

Dick mashed the potatoes. Bob filled our glasses with cold milk and put Brad into the highchair. A thick Los Angeles phone book was slipped under Chuckie. When everyone sat down, the table looked like a Norman Rockwell painting only with more Tupperware.

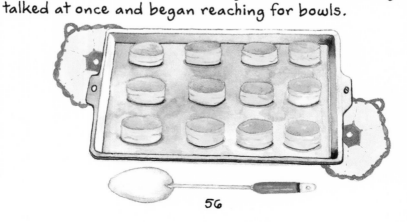

It was all there: the large platter with drumsticks and piles of sliced turkey, the big yellow bowl of Grandma's stuffing with the red-handled spoon, the dented pot of steaming mashed potatoes, a pitcher of gravy, sliced, jellied cranberry sauce (still showing the ridges from the can), cereal bowls of black olives, and celery stuffed with cream cheese, fruit salad, Jell-O salad, peas, and creamed onions. And, almost as important as the turkey, my grandma's hot homemade, floury biscuits wrapped in one of my great-grandma's embroidered flour-sack dish towels. The tree lights glowed, the house was cozy with the mingled smells of roast turkey and the pan of apple crisp that was baking in the oven. Everyone talked at once and began reaching for bowls.

56

"Wait a minute," my mom called out over the commotion. "Kids, put the bowls down. Let's say grace." She reached for Chuckie's hand. "Everyone hold hands. Sue take Bradley's hand." (We thought our mom made us hold hands so no one could get the food while our eyes were closed!) We linked hands until our circle was complete, bowed our heads and said the words with my dad ~ words from a much-loved hymn my grandmother had turned into a grace that tied us together as a family in sacred celebration of all we had and all we were to each other:

For the beauty of the earth,
for the glory of the skies,
For the love which from our birth
Over and around us lies,
Lord of all, to thee we raise
This, our hymn of grateful praise.

God Bless our Family. AMEN

Stephen said, "Don't forget Nipper! God bless Nipper!" Everyone laughed. Dad added with a smile, "But Nipper's family!" A discussion ensued between my brothers as to which one of them was Nipper's brother.

My dad looked at his family, seeing in their faces the past, present, and future, and laughed out loud. He walked around the table serving the turkey, asking, "Dark meat or white?"

Jim elbowed Steve and said, "Look!" and showed him his finger with an olive stuck on the end ⁓ which he instantly popped into his mouth. Steve's eyes lit up ⁓ he reached for the olives ⁓ and so it went, until both of them had olives on all their fingers. You might not know it, but we'd been practicing our manners at dinnertime since before Thanksgiving. We said please and thank you, chewed with our mouths closed, used our napkins, and ate olives off our fingers.

I'm sure Christmas dinner is where comfort food got its name. The first forkful of my grandmother's dressing, drenched in my mother's gravy, was pure Christmas ambrosia. Eyes rolled. My uncles' plates were heaped to the ceiling because they were still "growing boys." We thanked Mom and Grandma with smacking lips and told them they were the best cooks in the world. Second helpings went around. At the end, there was hot apple crisp with ice cream, pumpkin pie, and mince pie with whipped cream. Everyone had everything. It was a celebration of gratitude, because that's what we had.

♪ There's a happy feeling nothing in the world can buy
When they pass around the coffee and the pumpkin pie... ♪

We all ate ourselves into a coma ⁓ Dad and the uncles had to lie down and take a nap.

Later that night, after the table was cleared, the dishes were washed and dried and back in the cupboard ~ while turkey bones were simmering in the stock pot, and the wish bone was drying, we scavenged through the leftovers and did it all again. Turkey, piled on split and buttered biscuits, with a scoop of dressing, all of it doused in gravy. ᴍᴍᴍᴍᴍᴍ .♡

Before bed I put on my new jammies and went outside to our front porch. It was dark and the neighborhood was settling in for the night. Soft homey sounds were coming from the houses: the clattering of dishes, a baby crying, a dog barking. Lights began going off. Silvery smoke rose from chimneys and lightly spiced the air. My mom came outside to check on me.

"Oh my, it's beautiful out here." she said, "Look at that sky!"

I looked up. The stars sparkled so bright and seemed so close, they looked like they'd gotten caught in the tree branches. I leaned into my mom as she began showing me the constellations: the Big Dipper, the Little Dipper, the North Star, and Venus.

"And see that star right there?" she pointed. "That's the one I wished on to get you."

59

"You did? Oh, mom." It was a moment of infinite happiness. I might have grown 3 inches that night.

We watched a shooting star cross the sky leaving a trail of diamond dust.

"Look!" she said. "Hurry! Make a wish."

I closed my eyes, my heart so full of Christmas. I whispered the only thing I could think of which really wasn't a wish; it was the 3-word prayer my grandma taught me I could say anytime, "Thank you, God."

"Aren't we lucky?" Mom said, her arm hugging my shoulders. "What a dream. We'll remember this Christmas forever."

We stood looking at the sky a few minutes more, then she kissed the top of my head and said, "We should go in, it's been a big day. Time for bed."

followed her inside and kissed everyone goodnight. Dean Martin was singing *I'll Be Home for Christmas* on the record player.

said my prayers and shivered a little as I climbed into bed. My mom tucked my doll in next to me and mooshed the covers up around my ears the way I liked them. She held my face in her hands and told me she loves me. She left the bedroom door open a crack, and I listened to her footsteps disappear down the hall to the living room. I began to drift off to the comforting sounds of parents, Grandma and uncles talking quietly. When I closed my eyes, I saw a navy blue sky filled with stars and went to sleep dreaming of a world where every child believed in Santa, and every parent, too, and every day was Christmas, and every dream came true.

The End

AFTERWORD

As I got older and 1956 got further away, I couldn't wait to grow up and get my own house with my own kitchen, and a garden, and my own Christmas tree ~ where nobody could tell me what to do ~ I could eat chocolate cake for breakfast, turn the music up loud, and stay up all night if I wanted.

But now that I'm grown and have the whole story, I'd give anything for my mom to suddenly walk into the kitchen and say, "Time for bed, honey, it's been a big day." Tuck me in, moosh the covers around my ears, and tell me she loves me. That would be heaven.

This is the first book I've written that my dad didn't read first and give me his blessing with his highest compliment, "Ya did good." I'm being very brave publishing it anyway. He was my rock. He's still my rock.

Good dog

I was lucky to be one of eight children in the magical world our parents created. I've loved this extra time of being home for Christmas. It's been perfectly, as my mom would say, "dreamy."

I'll always feel you close to me
and though you're far from sight
I'll search for you among the stars
that shine on Christmas night.
♥ anon—.

Merry Christmas

Merry Christmas, everyone! Happy Hanukkah, Joyful Kwanzaa, Feliz Navidad, Joyeux Noel, and Season's Greetings to all. Here's to a healthy, peaceful, infinitely kind new year. 💙

Hours Fly
Flowers die
New days
New ways
Pass by
Love stays 💙

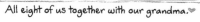

All eight of us together with our grandma. 💙

Know you what it is to be a child? It is to be very different from the man of today. It is to have a spirit still streaming from the waters of baptism; it is to believe in Love, to believe in Loveliness, to believe in belief; it is to be so little that the elves can reach to whisper in your ear...

♥ Francis Thompson

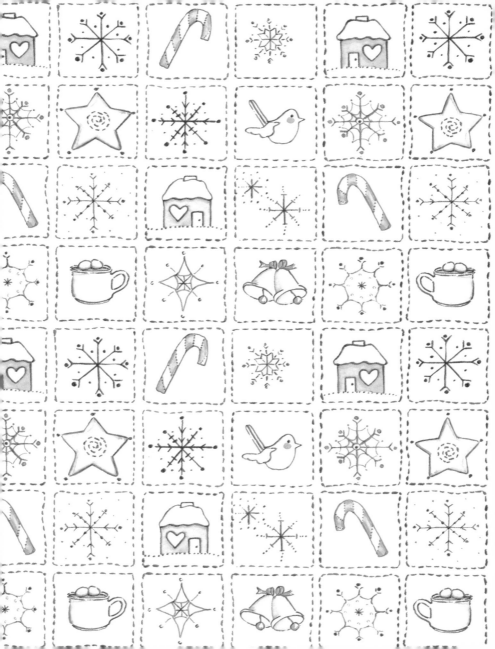

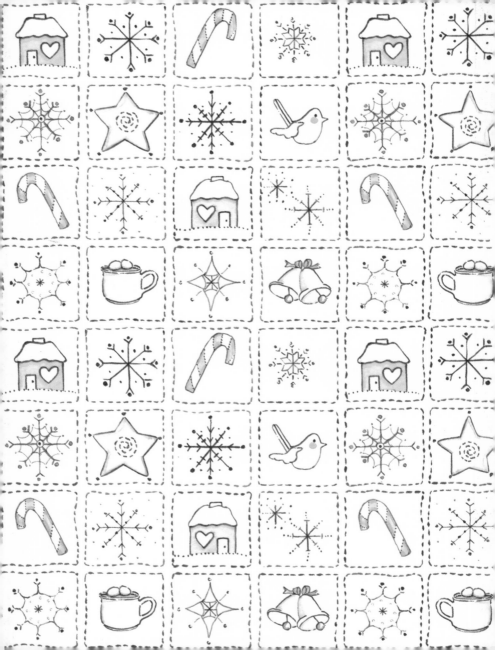